Tommy Goes to Harlem

Written by

Thomas St. Thomas

Illustrated by

Maria Savko

This book is dedicated to my children,
Lincoln and Tessa.

And with thanks to Thomas Sowell
for his unwavering dedication to truth.

A Children's Introduction to Thomas Sowell

Tommy Goes to Harlem

Written by
Thomas St. Thomas

Illustrated by
Maria Savko

This book is independently published by J. Thomas St. Thomas.

Tommy lived with his aunt and two older cousins. Like many families, they didn't have electricity or running water, but they had what counts. They had each other and a home full of love.

He didn't know that things were about to change in a big way, which would put him on a path to numerous adventures.

Tommy and his family left their town of Gastonia, North Carolina, and headed for Harlem, New York.

He would soon be introduced to a whole new world he never knew existed.

Harlem was very different than what Tommy was used to in Gastonia.

He had never seen such busy streets full of cars and double decker buses, or so many people and buildings all crammed so close together.

COTTON CLUB
COTTON CLUB
COTTON CLUB
COTTON
1222
1222
SPECIAL

Tommy quickly learned how to safely
cross a street and even how to ride
buses all by himself.

Being in a new city and far away
from old friends, it was time to find
some new ones.

PATSY
9 10 15
BK
SEAFOOD
LUNCH
OPTIMO
CIGARS

NEW YORK
PUBLIC LIBRARY

Making new friends in a new place can be tough, but Tommy's family knew a smart young boy named Eddie.

Eddie was kind enough to take Tommy to the local library and introduce him to the world of books.

Tommy was overwhelmed and amazed. He didn't know so many books existed in the world, much less in one building.

What could he buy with no money? He didn't know that libraries let you borrow books, so Eddie taught him all about it.

Eddie showed Tommy how to get a library card and borrow some books. Free of charge!

Tommy continued reading for years to come. All that reading would eventually pay off.

Tommy became the first person in his family to pass the 6th grade.

He was just getting started on his educational journey, but there would be some bumps along the way.

Being a teenager was tough. His family didn't understand why he spent so much time at the library, and he eventually dropped out of high school.

Little did he know being drafted into the Marine Corps would help him find his passion in life.

Taking pictures for the Marine Corps, he learned about the idea of trade-offs.

Focusing on any one thing will make the rest of the world seem blurry. People only have so much attention.

After Tommy's time in the Marine Corps, he had much more to do. His love of reading and studying was put to good use.

He spent several years studying economics in college. Economics helps us understand how people make decisions about the money they spend and how they use their talents.

Tommy also wanted to travel the world and learn about culture. Culture is a word we use to describe people's habits, attitudes, and traditions.

People in different places have different cultures where they practice different traditions. We all choose to focus on different things.

Tommy eventually became Dr. Thomas Sowell. He spent the rest of his life writing down those lessons in many, many books.

Those books are now in libraries across the world, just like the library his old friend Eddie introduced him to. There they sit, waiting for curious young people to learn those same lessons.